An Autumn Day

This book belongs to:

....

Off down the lane, Tractor Ted and Midge head.

The leaves on the trees
Have turned orange and red.

The tractors are busy
Harvesting crops.

At this time of year
There is no time to stop.

Potatoes are lifted
Up out of the ground.

They drop in the trailer
With a *tumbling*
sound.

A seed drill is planting Out a new crop.

"Here comes the harvester," Tractor Ted calls.

"Quick, quick," Midge shouts.
What can she see?

It's a small prickly hedgehog
Eating blackberries for tea.

"That makes me feel hungry! Let's go now," Midge says.

As they reach the farmhouse, Midge can see

A nice bowl of food
Left out for her tea!